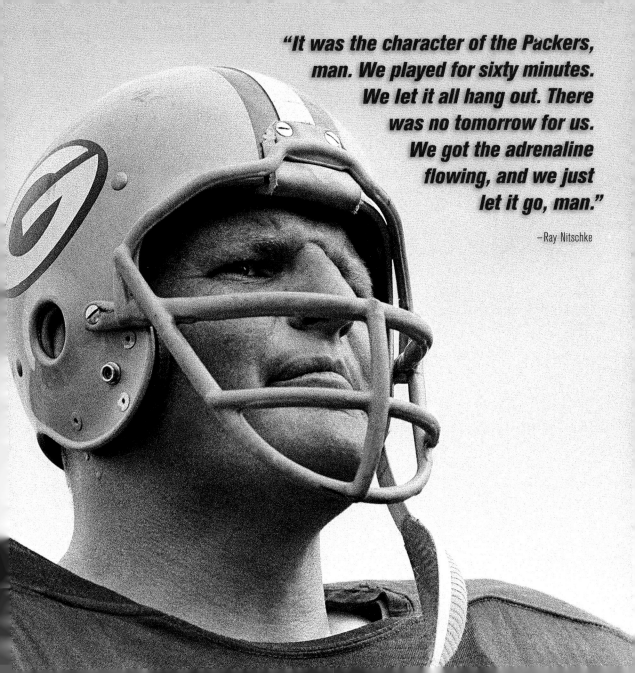

"It was the character of the Packers, man. We played for sixty minutes. We let it all hang out. There was no tomorrow for us. We got the adrenaline flowing, and we just let it go, man."

–Ray Nitschke

**DAVID GREEN**

**Stewart, Tabori & Chang**
**New York**

# 101 REASONS TO LOVE THE
# PACKERS

# INTRODUCTION

My earliest memories of the NFL hark back to the mid-1960s and the great teams of the Lombardi era. When I wasn't collecting baseball cards, I was using every scraped together penny, nickel, and dime to buy packs of football cards. Bart Starr, Elijah Pitts, and Boyd Dowler were among my most cherished.

Although I grew up in Charlotte, North Carolina, a quiet southern town between the bustling NFL cities of Washington and Atlanta, the Green Bay Packers captured my interest. Why? Quite simply, they were the best.

I'm sure I watched many games on television as a youngster, but the first game I remember clearly is Green Bay's 35–10 win over the Kansas City Chiefs in Super Bowl I, on January 15, 1967—when I was seven years old. The following year, I got to see the Packers do it again, trouncing Oakland, 33–14, in Super Bowl II. I was hooked. They made it seem so easy.

But then time played its cruel hand, and the Packers faded into mediocrity just as I was forging what would become a lifelong bond.

And while my devotion waned during the ensuing years, as it tends to do in adolescence when someone or something new comes along, I never lost my love for the Packers. I kept hoping for that long-awaited return to glory.

Lynn Dickey and Don Majkowski did their best to rekindle the magic, but they just didn't get enough help. Then some guy no one had heard of, with a misspelled and mispronounced name, came along—Brett Favre, a fearless gunslinger with a cowboy swagger that was irresistible to all but a few. Suddenly, the Packers were relevant again. More than relevant—they were champions. And under the leadership of Mike McCarthy and Aaron Rodgers, that tradition continues.

For more than 90 years, this upstart team from the smallest market in professional sports—a team with the heart of a tenacious underdog and the pedigree of a true champion—has earned the steadfast love and devotion of its growing army of fans.

If you know anything about the Packers, you know that there are countless reasons to love them. Here are 101 to get you started.

Jim Taylor (31) rumbles through the
Kansas City defense during Super Bowl I.

Bart Starr (15) throws a pass versus Los Angeles, 1962.

# 1 TITLETOWN, USA

It's the unofficial nickname of Green Bay, and rightly so. The Packers' 13 NFL championships are the most by any franchise. Green Bay has claimed the title in 1929, 1930, 1931, 1936, 1939, 1944, 1961, 1962, and 1965; and won Super Bowls I, II, XXXI, and XLV, in the 1966, 1967, 1996, and 2010 seasons, respectively.

1929
1930
1931
1936
1939
1944
1961
1962
1965
1966
1967
1996
2010

Tony Canadeo (3), Irv Comp (51), coach
Curly Lambeau, and Don Hutson (14)

# 2 21 HALL OF FAMERS

Green Bay boasts more Hall of Famers than any other franchise except the Chicago Bears. In order of induction, they are Curly Lambeau, Cal Hubbard, Don Hutson, Johnny "Blood" McNally (1963); Clarke Hinkle, Mike Michalske (1964); Arnie Herber (1966); Vince Lombardi (1971); Tony Canadeo (1974); Jim Taylor (1976); Forrest Gregg, Bart Starr (1977); Ray Nitschke (1978); Herb Adderley (1980); Willie Davis, Jim Ringo (1981); Paul Hornung (1986); Willie Wood (1989); Henry Jordan (1995); James Lofton (2003); and Reggie White (2006).

A game in 1923

# 3 BIRTH OF THE PACKERS

During the summer of 1919, Green Bay native and standout high school athlete Earl "Curly" Lambeau and *Green Bay Press-Gazette* sports editor George Calhoun discussed putting together a professional football team. Lambeau secured funding for uniforms from his employer, the Indian Packing Company, and Calhoun posted a notice in the *Press-Gazette* calling a meeting of all interested parties. A couple dozen players attended, electing Lambeau as captain.

It took a while to settle on a name. The Indians seemed like an obvious choice as a nod to the team's original sponsor. Calhoun often referred to them as the Big Bay Blue Boys in his articles. But Packers was the name that stuck, despite objections by both Lambeau and Calhoun. We'll never know if the Packers would have enjoyed the same level of success if Big Bay Blue Boys had caught on. Thank goodness it didn't.

# 4 YEAR ONE

Green Bay was a powerhouse from the first time the team set foot on the field, in 1919, obliterating Menominee North End, 53–0. The Packers went on to win nine more times that first year by lopsided scores like 87–0 and 85–0. On the season, Green Bay outscored its opponents 565–12 and finished 10–1. The Packers' only loss came in the finale, when the Beloit Fairies—yes, the Fairies—edged them 6–0. Green Bay scored the tying touchdown on three consecutive plays at the end of the game, but the referee—perhaps affected by some magic Fairy dust—called penalties on each of the plays, nullifying the scores.

# 5 CURLY LAMBEAU

As a freshman at Notre Dame, Lambeau played fullback under rookie coach Knute Rockne. After contracting a severe case of tonsillitis, Lambeau returned home, and once he recovered, he went to work as a clerk at Indian Packing Company in Green Bay. When Lambeau and George Calhoun put together Green Bay's first team, Lambeau not only played halfback, he also took on the role of head coach—at the tender age of 21.

For 31 years, Lambeau served as the Packers' head coach, winning six championships during that span, including three straight in 1929–31 and five in 11 years. A pioneer of the passing game, Lambeau created dominant offenses, and his coaching theories helped revolutionize football. Summer training camps, daily practices, scouting, and film study were all part of Lambeau's regimen long before they became common practice throughout the league.

Lambeau's 226 wins (209 with Green Bay) are the fourth-highest all-time total in NFL history. He was inducted into the Pro Football Hall of Fame in 1963. A bronze statue of Lambeau stands in front of the stadium named in his honor.

# 6 MONEY WELL SPENT

In late November 1921, three collegiate footballers from the University of Notre Dame suited up for a Packers game in Chicago. One of the players, Hunk Anderson, was recognized by a few of the sportswriters in attendance. The league punished Green Bay by revoking its franchise for the 1922 season. Curly Lambeau pleaded his case before league officials, apologizing for the misguided incident, and contributed $50 out of his own pocket to buy back the franchise, part of the newly reorganized and renamed National Football League. It turned out to be a very wise investment.

Curly Lambeau

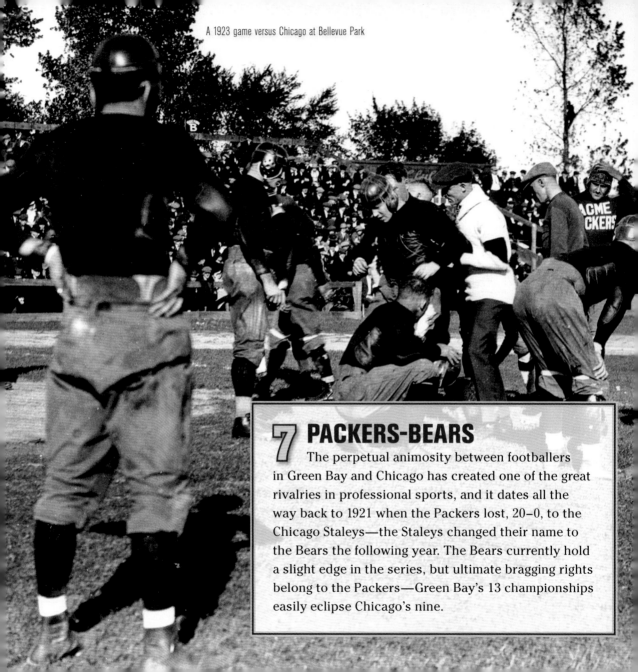

A 1923 game versus Chicago at Bellevue Park

# 7 PACKERS-BEARS

The perpetual animosity between footballers in Green Bay and Chicago has created one of the great rivalries in professional sports, and it dates all the way back to 1921 when the Packers lost, 20–0, to the Chicago Staleys—the Staleys changed their name to the Bears the following year. The Bears currently hold a slight edge in the series, but ultimate bragging rights belong to the Packers—Green Bay's 13 championships easily eclipse Chicago's nine.

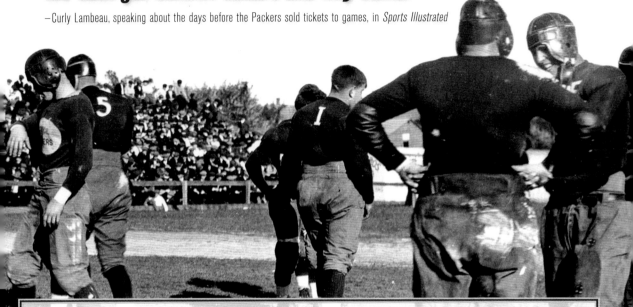

"We put the take from each gate into a bag and stowed it in a safe. At the end of the season we split the pot. We each got sixteen dollars and fifty cents."

—Curly Lambeau, speaking about the days before the Packers sold tickets to games, in *Sports Illustrated*

## 8 BEFORE LAMBEAU FIELD

The Packers originally played at Hagemeister Park in a vacant lot next to East High School in Green Bay. There were no seats. Spectators moved up and down the sidelines with the action or sat in their cars nearby. Admission was free, but a hat was usually passed to collect money for the team. In 1920, bleachers seating a few hundred fans were installed, and in 1921 the team started charging admission. When the parkland became the site of a new high school, the Packers spent a brief time playing at Bellevue Park, the local baseball stadium. Then, in 1925, more than 5,000 fans showed up for the first game at the original City Stadium, built behind the new East High. As the team's popularity grew, City Stadium was eventually expanded to seat 25,000. It would remain the Packers' home until 1957.

# 9 HOMEGROWN, PUBLICLY OWNED

In 1923, with the Packers organization struggling to remain solvent, Curly Lambeau joined with four prominent members of the Green Bay community—Gerald Clifford, Lee Joannes, Dr. W. Webber Kelly, and A. B. Turnbull—to form a group charged with keeping the franchise afloat. Nicknamed "the Hungry Five" by sportswriter Oliver Kuechle, these men guided the organization through early financial troubles, forming the Green Bay Football Corporation. Today, the Packers are the only major sports franchise that is non-profit and publicly owned. Shares of stock, which were first sold in 1923 for $5 each, pay no dividends and cannot be resold, but come with the pride of being an owner of an NFL team.

# 10 THREE-PEAT

The Packers are the only team in NFL history to win the league championship three consecutive years—twice. Green Bay first won three straight titles from 1929 to 1931, when Curly Lambeau's teams went a combined 34–5–2, winning eight or more games in a row three times. The best of those was the 1929 squad. That year, Green Bay outscored its opponents 198–22, including eight shutouts, while going 12–0–1.

The Packers and Lions battle, in 1930.

# 11 NEW BLOOD

In the off-season between 1928 and 1929, Curly Lambeau signed three veterans—Johnny "Blood" McNally, "Iron Mike" Michalske, and Cal Hubbard— to bolster an already solid Packers roster.

McNally, who played pro ball under the alias Johnny Blood while still in college, was a standout player on both sides of the ball, excelling at running back, receiver, and punter. He led the team in rushing in 1929 with 406 yards and scored a league-best 14 touchdowns in 1931.

Michalske, known as "Iron Mike" for his incredible durability, was a dominant force on both the offensive and defensive lines, particularly as a pass rusher. Iron Mike played eight seasons in Green Bay between 1929 and 1937, while wearing nine different numbers. It's not clear why Michalske changed so much, but it didn't matter. He made sure the opposition found him—rather, he found them.

At 6-2 and 250 pounds, Hubbard was one of the biggest players of his day—an anchor in Green Bay's great offensive lines of the era. After football, Hubbard began umpiring American League baseball games and eventually became the league's director of umpires.

All three were inducted into the Pro Football Hall of Fame. Hubbard is the only person to be a member of both the Pro Football and Baseball Halls of Fame.

Johnny McNally

Cal Hubbard

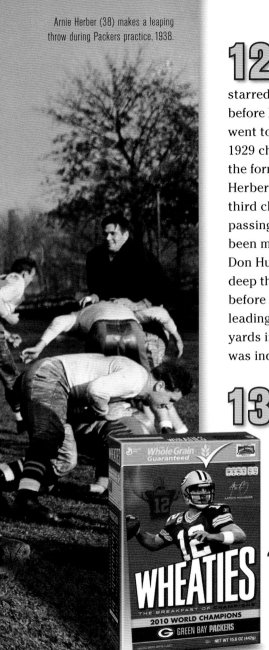

## 12 THE HANDYMAN

Arnie Herber was born and raised in Green Bay. He starred at West High School in both football and basketball before heading off to college. When he returned home, Herber went to work for the Packers as a handyman. Following the 1929 championship season, Curly Lambeau decided to give the former prep star a tryout, and Herber made the team. With Herber playing tailback, the Packers won their second and third championships in 1930 and 1931. Herber led the NFL in passing three times, in 1932, 1934, and 1936, and it might have been more if the NFL had kept statistics prior to 1932. When Don Hutson arrived in 1935, Herber had the game's first great deep threat, and the two created a formidable combo not seen before in the NFL. Herber threw for 1,239 yards in 1936 while leading the Packers to another title and tallied 1,107 passing yards in 1939—Green Bay's fifth championship season. Herber was inducted into the Pro Football Hall of Fame in 1966.

## 13 BREAKFAST OF CHAMPIONS

Wheaties is known as "the Breakfast of Champions." Cereal maker General Mills has featured Packers on the box several times, including Bart Starr (1964), the Super Bowl XXXI champs (1997), Brett Favre (1998), and, most recently, Aaron Rodgers and Clay Matthews in 2011.

*"We've got the best fans, and I can't wait to go home and see those fans and bring home the Lombardi Trophy."*

–Aaron Rodgers

## 14 CLARKE HINKLE

Few players were as tough as Hinkle. As a running back, Hinkle bulldozed opposing defenders, rushing for 3,860 yards over the course of his 10-year career, from 1932 to 1941. Hinkle led the Packers in rushing seven times, tying him with Jim Taylor for the most in Green Bay history. His 58 points scored in 1938 led the NFL. As a linebacker, Hinkle flattened backs and receivers with crushing hits. Chicago great Bronko Nagurski ran roughshod over most defenders, but not Hinkle—one of the few men able to bring down Nagurski on his own. And if that wasn't enough, Hinkle also handled the Packers' placekicking and punting duties. Hinkle was inducted into the Pro Football Hall of Fame in 1964.

## 15 MILWAUKEE'S BEST

From 1933 to 1994, the Packers played one to three of their home games in Milwaukee each season. They were 106–60–3 in those contests.

## 16 KROLL'S

Kroll's is a Green Bay landmark. The original restaurant opened in 1936 on Main Street in downtown Green Bay, and Kroll's West, which sits directly across Ridge Road from Lambeau Field, has been there since 1974. On game days, the restaurant may serve as many as 6,000 fans. Inside, the "Signature Wall" displays autographs of many Packers greats. But it's the legendary hamburgers and other charcoal-grilled specialties that keep devotees coming back.

## 17 THE ALL-NAME TEAM

Here are just a few of the colorful names that have graced the Packers roster through the years: Cub Buck, Jug Earp, Boob Darling, Bo Molenda, Jab Murray, Buford "Baby" Ray, Lavvie Dilweg, Beattie Feathers, Moose Gardner, Pid Purdy, Cowboy Wheeler, Whitey Woodin, Wimpy Winther, Elbert Bloodgood, Tiny Engebretsen, Elijah Pitts, Zeke Bratkowski, Na'il Diggs, T. J. Slaughter, R-Kal Truluck, Clyde Goodnight, Waldo Don Carlos, Mossy Cade, Chukie Nwokorie, and Kabeer Gbaja-Biamila.

Fans fill Kroll's parking lot prior to a Packers game.

Don Hutson

# 18 DON HUTSON

Back in 1993, *Sports Illustrated* columnist Peter King declared Hutson the best receiver ever. That's right, EVER. In 11 seasons, from 1935 to 1945, Hutson caught 99 TD passes, a record at the time. He led the league in total receptions eight times and touchdown receptions nine times. Both records still stand. In all, Hutson held 18 NFL records when he retired.

Hutson's athleticism and route running, combined with coach Curly Lambeau's innovations, changed the passing game, and thus changed football. The Packers became an offensive force unlike any other at the time, winning three NFL titles during Hutson's tenure, in 1936, 1939, and 1944.

Twice, in 1941 and 1942, Hutson was named the NFL's most outstanding player, and he was a consensus All-Pro five times. In addition to his offensive prowess, like most players of his era, Hutson played defense and kicked. His 823 points, including seven field goals and 172 extra points, were a Packers record until 2003.

And to think, Hutson very nearly never became a Packer. Both Green Bay and Brooklyn offered him contracts after Hutson completed his collegiate career at Alabama. League president Joe Carr awarded contractual rights to the Packers on his determination that the Packers' offer was postmarked just 17 minutes earlier than Brooklyn's. God bless the Postal Service.

In 1951, the Packers retired Hutson's number, 14. He was inducted into the Pro Football Hall of Fame in 1963, and in 1994 the Packers named their new state-of-the-art practice facility in honor of Hutson, continuing the legacy of one of the greatest ever to play the game.

*"Hutson invented modern pass receiving. He created Z-outs, buttonhooks, hook-and-gos, and a whole catalog of moves and fakes."*

—ProFootbalHOF.com

# 19 PACK O' PICKS

In a 27–6 win over the Detroit Lions on October 24, 1943, the Packers set an NFL record for interceptions in a game with nine. Don Hutson had two picks. Charley Brock, Tony Canadeo, Irv Comp, Bob Flowers, Charles Goldenberg, Joe Laws, and Andy Uram had the others.

# 20 LION TAMER

Facing Detroit in Milwaukee on October 7, 1945, Don Hutson grabbed four touchdown receptions and kicked five PATs, scoring an NFL-record 29 points—in the second quarter! That was more than enough to tame the toothless Lions. With some help from his teammates, Hutson and the Packers trounced Detroit, 57–21.

# 21 THE GRAY GHOST

Tony Canadeo, nicknamed "the Gray Ghost of Gonzaga" for his prematurely gray hair, led the Packers in rushing for four consecutive seasons, from 1946 to 1949. Canadeo became only the third back in NFL history to rush for more than 1,000 yards in a season, gaining 1,052 yards in 1949—on a team that went 2–10. Although he missed part of the 1944 season and all of 1945 while serving in the military, Canadeo's 4,197 total rushing yards rank him fourth all-time in the Packers' record book. A versatile competitor who also punted and made nine interceptions on defense, Canadeo called it quits in 1952, and his number, 3, was retired by the Packers. Canadeo was inducted into the Pro Football Hall of Fame in 1974.

Don Hutson, left, and Cecil Isbell
Inset: Tony Canadeo

## 22 JIM RINGO

Ringo left his first Packers training camp when he didn't think he was big enough to compete for the center's job. Fortunately for the Packers, he returned, and Ringo went on to become a Hall of Famer. Although he was small for his position, Ringo's speed, agility, and intelligence made him a dominating lineman. From 1954 to 1967, Ringo never missed a game. While in Green Bay, he was named All-Pro and selected for the Pro Bowl seven times. So it was no surprise when he got the call from the Pro Football Hall of Fame, in 1981.

Jim Ringo blocks the Colts' Dick Szymanski (36) as Jim Taylor (31) scores a touchdown, 1960.

# 23 THE ONE-EYED BANDIT

Free safety Bobby Dillon holds the team record for career interceptions with 52. In a remarkable stretch from 1953 to 1958, Dillon made 47 interceptions, five of which he returned for touchdowns. Four of his picks came in one game in 1953, a Thanksgiving Day contest won by the Detroit Lions, 34–15, despite Dillon's extraordinary efforts. Think that's incredible? How about this: Dillon had sight in only one eye. He lost the other in a childhood accident. Now that's amazing.

*"It's just the way it was, so it never bothered me when I was playing."*

—Bobby Dillon, on his eye injury

# 24 LAMBEAU FIELD

So many of the NFL's best have battled on this turf, the hallowed ground known as Lambeau Field. So many moments have become history at the Packers' longtime home. Built in a classic bowl shape, City Stadium opened in 1957 and was renamed Lambeau Field following the death of legendary coach and franchise cofounder Curly Lambeau, in 1965. It is the longest continuously occupied stadium in the NFL.

Several expansions have boosted Lambeau's capacity to more than 73,000 fans. A major renovation from 2001 to 2003 added the Lambeau Field Atrium and the Robert E. Harlan Plaza, named in honor of the former team CEO. Fourteen-foot-tall bronze statues of Curly Lambeau and Vince Lombardi greet fans as they enter the stadium from the plaza. Inside the atrium are the Packers Pro Shop, restaurants, meeting and event facilities, and the 25,000-square-foot Packers Hall of Fame. Among the numerous exhibits featured in the Hall of Fame are a re-creation of Vince Lombardi's office, lockers of all 21 Hall of Famers, and four Super Bowl trophies—with room for several more.

## 25 THE PACKERS FAN HALL OF FAME

In 1998, the Packers became the first NFL team to establish a hall of fame for fans. Each year, one fan is chosen as the ultimate Packers fan from hundreds of nominees. The charter member is Mel Knoke, who attended games for more than 70 years, first buying four season tickets in 1927. Each winner has his or her name displayed in the Packers FAN Hall of Fame and receives a bounty of gifts, including four club seats to Packers home games.

## 26 GREEN PIECE

Among the more than 300 Packers artifacts in the Pro Football Hall of Fame is a box of sod from Lambeau Field.

## 27 BETTER CHEDDAR

It's hardly surprising that brats are a popular concession item at Lambeau Field. You can even get brat pizza. But perhaps the most unusual offering is "traditional cheese curds": deep-fried chunks of local Wisconsin cheddar—a little taste of heaven.

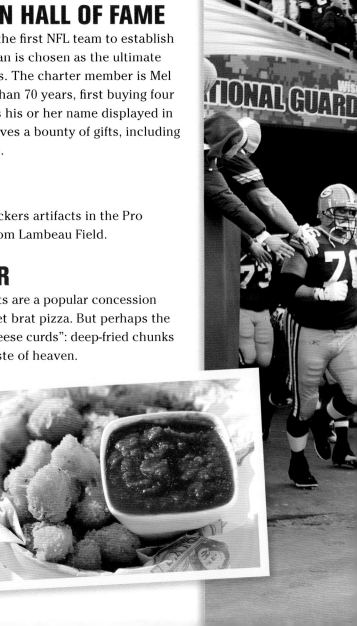

> *"Taking down the fried cheese curds w/sauce at Lambeau. I might be sleeping by game time."*
>
> —Darren Rovell, CNBC

Far right: Packers enter Lambeau Field from the players' tunnel, 2012.
Inset: Fried cheese curds

# 28 WALKING AMONG LEGENDS

To preserve a piece of Lambeau Field history when the Packers began a three-year stadium renovation/expansion project in 2001, head coach and GM Mike Sherman had three slabs of concrete that were part of the original players' tunnel from the locker room to the field moved and installed in the new tunnel. Now current and future Packers can make their entrance on the same walkway that all the great Packers of the past trod upon.

## 29 GREEN AND GOLD

Believe it or not, the Packers originally wore blue and gold, not green and gold. Blue and gold were the colors in the Indian Packing Company's logo as well as the colors of Curly Lambeau's alma mater, Notre Dame. Although the team sometimes wore green and gold during the 1930s and '40s, Green Bay didn't permanently switch to the now iconic green and gold combo until around 1950.

## 30 THE G LOGO

The Packers have utilized a few different "official" logos over the years, but only one, the current trademark "G" logo, ever made it to the helmet. The classic oval was designed by Packers equipment manager Gerald "Dad" Braisher at Vince Lombardi's request, in 1961.

## 31 BLOOD MONEY

Jim Becker didn't have the money to purchase season tickets back in 1952, so he started giving blood once every three months, collecting $15 or so for each pint he donated. Later, he found out it may have saved his life. In 1975, Becker was diagnosed with hemochromatosis, a potentially fatal condition in which the body absorbs too much iron. The treatment is to give blood regularly to control the level of iron in the bloodstream. Thanks to his love of the Packers, Becker already was doing just that. Becker was inducted into the Packers FAN Hall of Fame in 2010.

## 32 JUST WAIT

Season tickets to Packers home games have sold out every year since 1960. The waiting list now has more than 90,000 names on it. The estimated wait for those recently added to the list is about 850 years.

## 33 1958 NFL DRAFT

In 1958, head coach Scooter McLean drafted linebackers Dan Currie (1st) and Ray Nitschke (3rd), fullback Jim Taylor (2nd), and offensive guard Jerry Kramer (4th). Green Bay finished the season 1–10–1 under McLean, the team's worst record in Packers history, and McLean resigned. But the players he drafted that year became the foundation of Green Bay's dynasty during the 1960s.

Scooter McLean and Packers scout
Jack Vainisi at the 1958 NFL Draft

Ray Nitschke

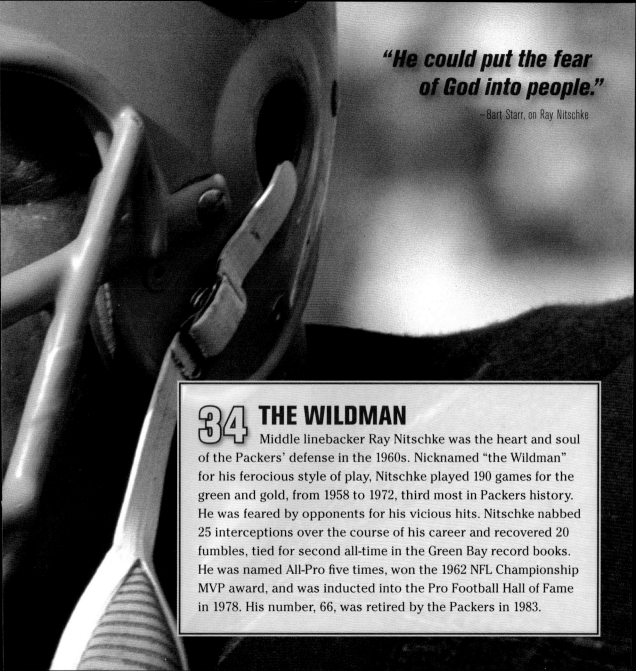

> **"He could put the fear of God into people."**
>
> – Bart Starr, on Ray Nitschke

## 34 THE WILDMAN

Middle linebacker Ray Nitschke was the heart and soul of the Packers' defense in the 1960s. Nicknamed "the Wildman" for his ferocious style of play, Nitschke played 190 games for the green and gold, from 1958 to 1972, third most in Packers history. He was feared by opponents for his vicious hits. Nitschke nabbed 25 interceptions over the course of his career and recovered 20 fumbles, tied for second all-time in the Green Bay record books. He was named All-Pro five times, won the 1962 NFL Championship MVP award, and was inducted into the Pro Football Hall of Fame in 1978. His number, 66, was retired by the Packers in 1983.

# 35  VINCE WHO?

Dominic Olejniczak, Packers president from 1958 to 1982, took charge of the search for a new head coach following the Packers' miserable 1–10–1 season in 1958 and made perhaps the biggest decision in the history of the organization. Olejniczak recommended a little-known New York Giants assistant coach, Vince Lombardi, for the job—and we all know how that turned out. Olejniczak was inducted into the Green Bay Packers Hall of Fame in 1979.

# 36  VINCE LOMBARDI

Quite simply, Lombardi is the greatest coach in the history of the game. Hired by the Packers to resurrect the stumbling franchise, Lombardi came to Green Bay with no prior head coaching experience. Lombardi's highly disciplined approach instilled a much-needed confidence in the players that immediately showed on the field. Behind a relentless ground attack and bruising defense, the Packers reversed course in 1959, and finished the season with a 7–5 record. An 8–4 record in 1960 won the Western Conference title, but the Packers fell to the Philadelphia Eagles 17–13 in the title game. It was the first and last playoff game Lombardi would lose as head coach.

Over the next seven years, Green Bay won five NFL titles and the first two Super Bowls, in 1966 and 1967. Lombardi, who also served as general manager, compiled an 89–29–4 regular season record in nine seasons in Green Bay. His teams were an incredible 9–1 in the playoffs. A 14-foot-tall bronze statue of Lombardi stands in the plaza outside Lambeau Field. He was inducted posthumously into the Pro Football Hall of Fame in 1971.

Vince Lombardi with his players

"He was the best coach ever, and I think few would question or argue that."

—Jerry Kramer, on Vince Lombardi

# 37 IN LOMBARDI'S WORDS
Here are a few memorable quotes from Vince Lombardi:

**"We would accomplish many more things if we did not think of them as impossible."**

**"Perfection is not attainable, but if we chase perfection we can catch excellence."**

**"Show me a good loser, and I'll show you a loser."**

**"The greatest accomplishment is not in never falling, but in rising again after you fall."**

**"The measure of who we are is what we do with what we have."**

**"The only place success comes before work is in the dictionary."**

**"The price of success is hard work, dedication to the job at hand, and the determination that whether we win or lose, we have applied the best of ourselves to the task at hand."**

**"Winners never quit and quitters never win."**

Vince Lombardi is carried off the field on the shoulders of Jim Taylor, left, and Paul Hornung after Green Bay's 23-12 victory over Cleveland, January 2, 1966.

*"I've got permanent wrinkles just from smiling for photos."*

—Saint Vince

Saint Vince and Cheese Louise
Inset: Kabeer Gbaja-Biamila greets fans
as he rides a bike to training camp.

# 38 SAINT VINCE

Packers superfan John O'Neill from Middleton, Wisconsin, is lovingly known as "Saint Vince." O'Neill attends Packers games regaled in a shimmering green bishop's robe trimmed in gold and a miter featuring a photo of Vince Lombardi atop his head. His wife, Mary Beth Johnson, also known as "Cheese Louise," prefers a faux-cheese bikini top to Saint Vince's formal attire—weather permitting, of course.

# 39 BIKING TO WORK

One of the great traditions of Packers training camp involves players riding kids' bikes to practice. Begun by Vince Lombardi in the 1960s, young Packers fans are encouraged to line up with their bikes at the players' entrance to Lambeau Field, where players can then grab a bike and ride it across the street to the practice facility.

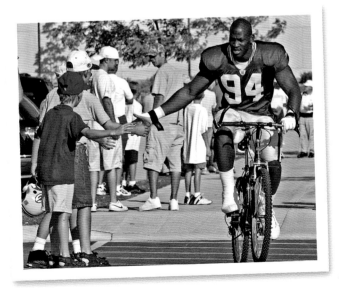

# 40 PAUL HORNUNG

The Heisman Trophy–winning "Golden Boy" out of Notre Dame was one of the most versatile athletes ever to play in Green Bay... or in the NFL, for that matter. Vince Lombardi installed Hornung as his left halfback in 1959, and Hornung went on to lead the league in scoring for three consecutive seasons, from 1959 to 1961. Hornung twice scored 30 or more points in a game, in 1961 and 1965. His 33 points versus Baltimore, on October 8, 1961, are a Packers record. In addition to 50 rushing touchdowns, including 13 in 1960, and 12 touchdown receptions, Hornung also converted 66 field goal attempts, kicked 190 extra points, and threw five touchdown passes over the course of his career. He ranks fourth all-time in scoring for Green Bay with 760 points. Despite these accomplishments, which also include the 1961 league MVP award, Hornung was not voted into the Pro Football Hall of Fame until the 15th ballot, in 1986.

Paul Hornung (5) dashes between defenders during a Packers scrimmage.

## 41 176

In 1960, Paul Hornung scored an NFL-record 176 points—in only 12 games. The total included 15 touchdowns, 15 field goals, and 41 PATs. The record lasted until 2006, when it was broken by San Diego's LaDainian Tomlinson, who scored 186 points—in 16 games.

## 42 JFK OK

New York Giants fans could not have been happy in 1961 when, at Vince Lombardi's request, President Kennedy granted Packers star halfback Paul Hornung leave from the Army to play in the NFL Championship Game on New Year's Eve. Hornung scored 19 points, tying a title game record, as the Packers demolished New York, 37–0. It was the first of five championships the Packers would win under Lombardi.

*"Paul Hornung isn't going to win the war on Sunday."*

–President John F. Kennedy

Paul Hornung rushes through the mud in the Packers' 17–9 victory over Detroit, 1961.

Jim Taylor leaps over a fallen
Pittsburgh defender in 1960.

# 43 JIM TAYLOR

Taylor was Vince Lombardi's workhorse, a back who could pound away at the defense—"Thunder" to the versatile Paul Hornung's "Lightning." Taylor's name is all over the Packers record book. He's second all-time in rushing yards (8,207) and attempts (1,811). His 4.53 yards per attempt is also second best in team history. Taylor's 81 career rushing touchdowns far surpass the record of any other Packer. For seven consecutive years, from 1960 to 1967, Taylor led the team in rushing. In five of those years, from 1960 to 1964, Taylor ran for more than 1,000 yards. His total of 1,474 yards rushing in 1962 led the league, and he was voted NFL Player of the Year. Taylor's performance in the bitterly cold 1962 title game versus the Giants is legendary. He rushed 31 times for 85 yards, scoring the contest's only offensive touchdown. When the game ended, Taylor was so battered and bruised, he couldn't talk and could barely see. The five-time Pro Bowler was elected to the Pro Football Hall of Fame in 1976.

## "He's tougher than Japanese arithmetic."

—Norm Van Brocklin, on Jim Taylor

Willie Wood (24) flips Oakland's Fred Biletnikov (25), 1970.
Left: Herb Adderley

## 44 WILLIE WOOD

A quarterback in college, Wood was signed by Green Bay as a free agent after going undrafted in 1960. Vince Lombardi converted Wood to safety, and he went on to become one of the best in NFL history. Wood played in every game from 1960 to 1971, earning Pro Bowl honors eight times. He led the Packers in interceptions five times and led the NFL in 1962 with nine picks. His 50-yard return of an interception in Super Bowl I was the turning point in the game. His 48 career interceptions rank second in the Packers record book. Wood was inducted into the Pro Football Hall of Fame in 1989.

## 45 HERB ADDERLEY

Adderley was another of Vince Lombardi's notable conversion projects. There was little opportunity for the rookie running back out of Michigan State to play behind Packers greats Jim Taylor and Paul Hornung, so Lombardi, needing a replacement for the injured Hank Gremminger, switched Adderley to cornerback, in 1961. Adderley excelled at the position, using his size and strength to his advantage against speedy receivers. In nine years in Green Bay, Adderley collected 39 interceptions, the most ever for a Packers corner, and his seven career interception returns for touchdowns set a record until Charles Woodson broke it in 2009. He also had a 60-yard interception return for a touchdown in Super Bowl II. As a kick returner, Adderley compiled a career average of 25.67 yards, fifth best all-time. His 3,080 total kickoff return yards, including a 103-yard touchdown return versus Baltimore in 1962, is third best in Packers history. Adderley was inducted into the Pro Football Hall of Fame in 1980.

### *"God didn't make a whole lot of Herb Adderleys."*

—Willie Wood

Jim Taylor (31) scores the Packers' only touchdown in the 1962 championship versus New York.

# 46 BEST EVER

It's tough to argue with folks who say the 1962 squad was the best Packers team ever. Green Bay went 13–1 that year, losing only to Detroit, on Thanksgiving Day, 26–14. The Packers won the first 10 games of the season, and they outscored opponents 415–148 for the year. Green Bay crushed both Chicago and Philadelphia by identical scores of 49–0. In the Philadelphia game, the Packers outgained the Eagles 628 yards to 54.

Green Bay won its second consecutive championship over the New York Giants, 16–7, in conditions that were brutal even by Green Bay standards—13 degrees with winds of 40 miles per hour. Television crews are said to have used nearby bonfires to thaw their cameras. Ray Nitschke earned game MVP honors, deflecting a pass that was then intercepted by Dan Currie and recovering two fumbles. Jim Taylor rushed for 85 yards on 31 carries and scored Green Bay's only touchdown. Jerry Kramer somehow converted three field goals in the arctic gale.

# 47 THE CLEVELAND CONNECTION

Defensive end Willie Davis and tackle Henry Jordan anchored the dominating Packers defensive lines of the 1960s that won five championships and two Super Bowls. Both came to Green Bay through trades with Cleveland. And both earned high praise for their speed, intelligence, and durability. Davis played in every Packers game from 1960 to 1969, while Jordan missed only two games from 1959 to 1968. Together they put seemingly relentless pressure on opposing quarterbacks. Davis may have held the Packers record for sacks had the statistic been kept at the time. His 21 fumble recoveries remain a Packers record. Both men were inducted into the Pro Football Hall of Fame—Davis in 1981 and Jordan in 1995.

# 48 THE KICK

Trailing 10–7 with less than two minutes to play in the 1965 Western Conference championship playoff game versus Baltimore, Packers kicker Don Chandler trotted out to attempt a 22-yard game-tying field goal. A gusting wind made the kick anything but routine. Chandler's attempt started down the middle, but the wind blew it over the right upright. Chandler reacted as if he had missed it. The Colts thought it sailed wide right (naturally), but referee Jim Tunney ruled that it passed over the goalpost before veering wide. The conversion tied the game, and the Packers went on to win 13–10 in overtime on a 25-yard Chandler field goal.

# 49 DAVE ROBINSON

Great players make big plays in big moments. That was Packers linebacker Dave Robinson. And his biggest moment came in the 1966 NFL Championship Game versus Dallas. Clinging to a 34–27 lead late in the game, the Packers needed a stop. Dallas had a fourth-and-goal from the Packers' 2. Robinson read pass and blitzed quarterback Don Meredith, drilling Meredith as he released the ball. The "wounded duck" fluttered softly into Packers safety Tom Brown's hands for a game-saving interception. The Packers went on to win Super Bowl I two weeks later. Robinson, who collected 21 interceptions in 10 seasons in Green Bay, from 1963 to 1972, played in three Pro Bowls. He was inducted into the Packers Hall of Fame in 1982.

Packers defenders pursue Cleveland's Jim Brown (32) in the 1965 championship game.

# 50 THREE-PEAT REPEAT

Vince Lombardi's Packers duplicated the 1929–31 team's trifecta, winning three consecutive titles from 1965 to 1967. A 10–3–1 record gave the Packers a share of the Western Conference title in 1965. After edging Baltimore 13–10 in the conference championship game, the Packers dispatched Cleveland 23–12 to win their ninth NFL title, holding the great Jim Brown to only 50 yards rushing in the game. Green Bay then went on to defeat the Dallas Cowboys in the NFL Championship Games in both 1966 and 1967 on their way to winning Super Bowls I and II.

# 51 THE PACKERS SWEEP

The sweep was Vince Lombardi's signature play. Both guards pulled and rumbled around the end, bulldozing a path for the running back who followed. The lead guard was responsible for blocking the cornerback, and the offside guard was responsible for the middle or outside linebacker. During the 1960s, guards Jerry Kramer and Fuzzy Thurston ran it to near perfection. From 1960 to 1964, the Packers averaged 169 yards rushing per game, including a team-record 196 yards per game in 1961. Although Kramer may be the most famous of all Packers linemen, he is the only member of the NFL's 50th Anniversary All-Time Team not to be named to the Pro Football Hall of Fame.

Elijah Pitts (22) follows guards Fuzzy Thurston
(63) and Jerry Kramer (64) on the famed Packers
Sweep during Super Bowl I.

Max McGee makes a juggling touchdown catch during Super Bowl I.

# 52 SIMPLY SUPER

With the kickoff of the first "Super Bowl" looming, backup receiver Max McGee claims he sneaked out of the team's hotel following bed check the night before the big game and played on little or no sleep after spending the evening entertaining a couple of stewardesses. Of course, McGee wasn't planning on getting a lot of playing time since he was behind star receiver Boyd Dowler on the depth chart. But when Dowler was injured on Green Bay's first series of the game, McGee stepped in.

McGee, who had only four receptions during the regular season, caught seven passes from Bart Starr for 138 yards in Super Bowl I, on January 15, 1967. Two of those catches went for touchdowns as the Packers pummeled Kansas City 35–10. The first was a spectacular one-handed grab that gave Green Bay a 7–0 lead in the first quarter. The second, a 13-yarder near the end of the third quarter, increased the Packers' lead to 28–10, sealing the Chiefs' fate.

Starr finished the day 16 of 23 for 250 yards and won the game's MVP award. McGee ended up in the broadcast booth after his playing days were over. He spent 20 years calling Green Bay games with partner Jim Irwin, finally calling it quits following the 1998 season.

### *"When it's third and ten, you can take the milk drinkers and I'll take the whiskey drinkers every time."*

—Max McGee

Bart Starr (15) scores the winning touchdown in the Ice Bowl.

# 53 THE ICE BOWL

It's the most famous game in NFL history. Period. December 31, 1967, Packers versus Cowboys in Green Bay for the NFC Championship. The temperature at game time was 13 degrees below zero with a wind chill of 46 below.

The field was frozen solid after the heating system failed. Some speculate that Packers coach Vince Lombardi simply turned it off, hoping to gain an advantage over the opponent from Dallas.

Two touchdown passes from Bart Starr to Boyd Dowler gave the Packers an early 14–0 lead. But a couple of Green Bay turnovers allowed Dallas to cut the lead to 14–10 at halftime. When Lance Rentzel hauled in an option pass from Dan Reeves and took it 50 yards for a touchdown on the first play of the fourth quarter, the Cowboys led 17–14.

With less than five minutes left, the Packers got one last chance. Starting from their own 32-yard line, Starr methodically drove his team down the frozen field. Faced with a third down at the Cowboys' 1 and only 16 seconds remaining, it was do-or-die time. Lombardi called a run up the gut by fullback Chuck Mercein, but concerned about the unpredictable footing, Starr elected to keep the ball. Behind the crushing blocks of guard Jerry Kramer and center Ken Bowman, Starr found just enough room to squeeze across the goal line for the game-winning touchdown. Not only was this a defining moment for the Packers, en route to another championship, but the game has become an iconic moment in football's grand history.

## *"Well, run it, and let's get the hell out of here."*

—Vince Lombardi to Bart Starr during a timeout before the game-winning quarterback sneak

# 54 MERCEIN'S MOMENT

Chuck Mercein's regular season rushing numbers in 1967 weren't impressive—14 carries for 56 yards. The backup fullback got little work, but when he was called upon to replace injured starter Jim Grabowski in the famed Ice Bowl, Mercein delivered. On the historic 12-play, 68-yard final drive, Mercein accounted for half of the yardage. His 19-yard catch and run to the Dallas 11 with a minute and a half left, followed by an 8-yard run to the Cowboys' 3, put Green Bay in scoring position. The final play called for a handoff to Mercein, but Bart Starr kept the ball and scored the game-winning touchdown. Still, it was Mercein who ended up on the cover of *Sports Illustrated* the following week, and rightfully so.

# 55 THE FROZEN TUNDRA

Lambeau Field was dubbed "the Frozen Tundra" following the Ice Bowl in 1967. It can be the coldest place on earth for teams visiting in January. Packers fans, of course, pride themselves on braving the most frigid temperatures—as well they should. After all, who wouldn't risk a bit of hypothermia for a chance to see a game at Lambeau?

# 56 CHEESEHEADS

The nickname that began as a disparaging term coined by Illinois fans in reference to their rivals in Wisconsin has been unconditionally embraced by Packers fans. The Cheesehead hat, originally designed by Wisconsinite Ralph Bruno, debuted at a Brewers–White Sox baseball game in 1987, but now it is worn proudly by thousands of Packers fans around the country.

# 57 BART STARR

Consider this: Starr led the Packers to five championships between 1961 and 1967—the most ever by a quarterback. He had a 9–1 record in the playoffs, losing only the 1960 NFL Championship—his first appearance in the postseason. Starr's teams won the first two Super Bowls, and he was MVP of both games. He led the NFL in passing three times and won league MVP honors in 1966. Starr's 57.4 completion percentage over 16 seasons was a league record when he retired in 1971. And Starr scored the winning touchdown in the Ice Bowl after driving his team 68 yards in the final five minutes of the historic 1967 NFL Championship Game. The Packers retired Starr's number, 15, in 1973, and Starr was elected to the Pro Football Hall of Fame in 1977. Not bad for a guy who wasn't drafted until the 17th round.

"For my money, he's the best quarterback of all time."

—Jim Taylor, on Bart Starr

Boyd Dowler (86) hauls in a Bart Starr touchdown pass against
Mel Renfro of the Dallas Cowboys, in the Ice Bowl.

## 58 BOYD DOWLER

Dowler, a third-round draft pick out of Colorado in 1959, had an immediate impact with the Packers. He won the NFL's Rookie of the Year award that year with 32 receptions for 549 yards and four touchdowns, and he was a key contributor throughout the dynasty years of the 1960s. Seven times in 11 seasons, Dowler led the team in receptions. His 6,918 total receiving yards are fifth best in Packers history. Dowler had two TD catches in the historic Ice Bowl, in 1967, and added a 62-yard touchdown catch in Super Bowl II. A two-time Pro Bowl selection, Dowler was inducted into the Packers Hall of Fame in 1978.

*"The only pressure we felt was to win a championship."*

—Boyd Dowler

Donny Anderson (44) bursts through the Oakland Raiders' defense, scoring a touchdown during Super Bowl II.

## 59 THE END OF AN ERA

Following Green Bay's historic win in the Ice Bowl, the Packers headed to the tropical warmth of Miami for Super Bowl II to face AFL champion Oakland. Most of the Packers knew coach Lombardi was likely retiring after the game, so it was paramount to them that his tenure come to a close with another championship. When Bart Starr connected with Boyd Dowler early in the second quarter for a 62-yard touchdown pass, Green Bay led 13–0. They were hardly threatened from there as the Packers cruised to a 33–14 victory. Starr won his second straight Super Bowl MVP. Don Chandler contributed four field goals, Willie Davis had three sacks, and Herb Adderley returned an interception 60 yards for a score. Lombardi retired as coach two weeks later but remained as GM. With the bittersweet victory, the Packers' fifth title in seven years brought an end to one of the great eras in sports history.

## 60 THE LOMBARDI TROPHY

A few months after Vince Lombardi's death, in 1970, prior to Super Bowl V, NFL Commissioner Pete Rozelle paid the ultimate tribute to Green Bay's legendary coach: Rozelle had the Super Bowl championship trophy renamed the Vince Lombardi Trophy, immortalizing the Packers icon.

# 61 FORREST GREGG

Gregg is considered the best right tackle ever to play in Green Bay. From 1956 to 1970, Gregg anchored the right side of the Packers' offensive line, earning All-Pro honors eight times, and was selected to play in the Pro Bowl nine times. He was considered the NFL's "iron man," playing in a then record 188 consecutive games from 1956 to 1971. All but one of those games was with the Packers. Gregg returned to coach the Packers in 1984, but to say that he failed to connect with his players is a huge understatement. He was dismissed in 1987. Gregg was inducted into the Pro Football Hall of Fame in 1977.

# 62 MANY HAPPY RETURNS

In 1967, Travis Williams averaged more than 41 yards per kickoff return, an NFL record. Williams returned four kicks for touchdowns that year, including a 104-yarder versus the Rams—the second longest in Green Bay history behind Al Carmichael's 106-yard return, in 1956. Williams had two returns for touchdowns in a game against the Cleveland Browns, tying a league record.

# 63 THE MAD STORK

Ted Hendricks played only one of the 15 seasons of his Hall of Fame career in Green Bay, but he made it count. Known as "the Mad Stork" for his lanky, 6-foot-7-inch frame and his quirky personality, Hendricks blocked seven kicks in 1974, an NFL record.

## *"Forrest Gregg is the finest player I ever coached!"*

—Vince Lombardi

Travis Williams (23) avoids several Cleveland Browns defenders on his way to an 87-yard kickoff return, in 1967.

Head coach Bart Starr, right, shakes hands with kicker Chester Marcol (13) following Marcol's game-winning field goal, October 29, 1978, as holder Bobby Douglas, left, looks on.

## 64 PAUL COFFMAN

Coffman talked his way onto the team, convincing assistant coach John Meyer to give him a tryout while Meyer was visiting Kansas State to scout another player. The Packers then signed Coffman as a free agent after he went undrafted in 1978. In 1979, Coffman set a Packers record for receptions by a tight end with 56—a record that still stands. He caught 40 or more passes every season from 1979 through 1985, except the strike-shortened 1982 season. Coffman's 39 touchdown catches are the most ever by a Packers tight end. Coffman was elected to the Packers Hall of Fame in 1994.

## 65 SIMPLY MARCOLOUS

The overmatched Packers somehow held the powerful Bears in check in the 1980 season opener, forging a 6–6 tie at the end of regulation. In overtime, Green Bay drove deep into Bears territory and lined up for a potential game-winning 34-yard field goal attempt by kicker Chester Marcol, "the Polish Prince." Marcol's kick was low, smashing into the face mask of Bears' defensive tackle Alan Page and ricocheting right back to Marcol, who snatched it out of the air and scooted into the end zone untouched for a game-winning touchdown.

## 66 LYNN DICKEY

The Packers teams that Dickey led from 1976 to 1985 may not have been as successful as some others, but Dickey still managed to put up some huge passing numbers. His 4,458 total passing yards in 1983 were the best single season total in Packers history until 2011, when Aaron Rodgers broke Dickey's record. And his 418 yards passing versus Tampa Bay in 1980 was also a team record that lasted until 2011, when it was broken by Matt Flynn. Dickey ranks third all-time in career passing yards with 21,369. Three times he threw for more than 3,000 yards, in 1980, '83, and '84. His 9.21 yards per attempt in 1983 also set a team record. Dickey was inducted into the Packers Hall of Fame in 1992.

## 67 A TALE OF TWO HALVES

The Packers opened the 1982 season against the Los Angeles Rams, in Milwaukee. With a possible players strike looming, Green Bay came out flat and trailed 23–0 at halftime. But quarterback Lynn Dickey rallied the team, throwing three second-half touchdown passes, and the Packers stunned the Rams 35–23—the biggest comeback in team history.

## "People have no idea how tremendous Lynn was."

—Paul Coffman

# 68 THE DEFENSE RESTS

On October 17, 1983, the Packers hosted the Washington Redskins for a Monday night game at Lambeau Field. On paper, Washington was clearly the superior team, but not on this night. The game turned into a track meet, with neither defense able to consistently stop the other team. Washington quarterback Joe Theismann threw for 398 yards, and Green Bay's Lynn Dickey matched him with 387. In all, there were 1,025 yards of total offense.

With just 54 seconds left in the game, veteran Jan Stenerud kicked a 20-yard field goal to give the Packers a 48–47 lead. But this game wasn't over. The 'Skins had kicker Mark Moseley, the league's MVP in 1982, ready on the sideline, and they moved quickly into field goal range. Moseley had missed only one attempt the previous season and had made 82 percent of his kicks from inside 40 yards over the course of his career. But this time, he missed the 39-yarder as time expired and the fans at Lambeau Field exploded in celebration. The game became an instant classic.

# 69 JAMES LOFTON

Lofton, the speedy receiver with soft hands out of Stanford, was one of the best ever to don the green and gold. For nine consecutive years, from 1978 to 1986, Lofton led the team in receiving—his 9,656 career receiving yards set the Packers record until 2011, when it was broken by Donald Driver. Lofton tallied 100 or more yards receiving in 32 games, a Packers record, and topped 1,000 yards receiving in five different years. His 18.22 yards per reception is fourth best in Packers history. A seven-time Pro Bowler while with the Packers, Lofton was inducted into the Pro Football Hall of Fame in 2003.

James Lofton (80) celebrates a Packers victory with Mike Douglass (53).

"From 1988 to 1990, Don Majkowski was the biggest thing in Wisconsin since sliced cheese."

—Chuck Carlson, *Green Bay Packers: Yesterday & Today*

# 70 THE MAJIK MAN

Don Majkowski's 1989 season was "majikal." Nicknamed "Majik Man" for his heroics on the field, the 10th-round pick out of Virginia threw for 4,318 yards—fourth best in Packers history—and 27 touchdowns. Majkowski led the league in passing yards, finished second to Joe Montana in MVP voting, and was named to the Pro Bowl. The Packers went 10–6, winning four games by a single point, and just missed out on a playoff spot.

Majkowski will forever be remembered for his last-minute, game-winning 14-yard TD pass to Sterling Sharpe versus Chicago that year. The line judge initially ruled that Majkowski had stepped over the line of scrimmage before releasing the throw, but a review of the play overturned the ruling, allowing the play to stand. The resulting touchdown gave the Packers a 14–13 victory in what became known as "Instant Replay Game." It broke an eight-game losing streak against the Bears.

When Majkowski injured his ankle in a 1992 contest versus the Cincinnati Bengals, he was replaced by Brett Favre, beginning Favre's incredible streak of consecutive games played. Majkowski was inducted into the Packers Hall of Fame in 2005.

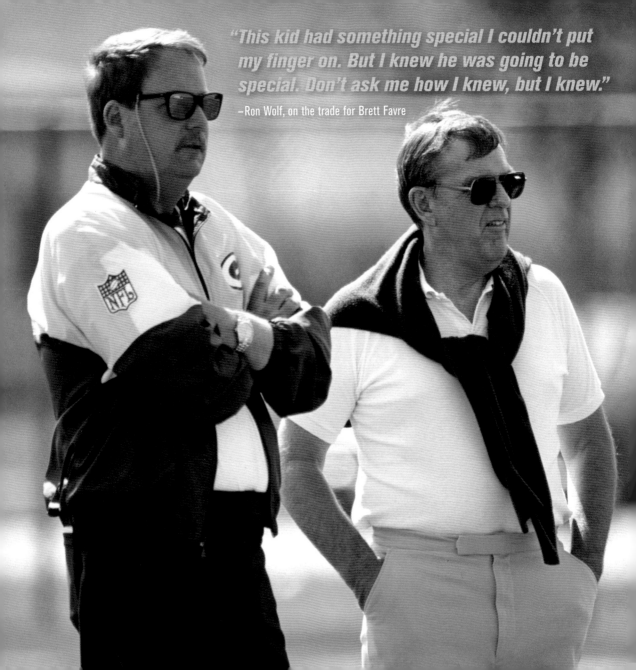

"This kid had something special I couldn't put my finger on. But I knew he was going to be special. Don't ask me how I knew, but I knew."

–Ron Wolf, on the trade for Brett Favre

# 71 RON WOLF

Five winning seasons in the previous 24 years—not a memorable time in Packers history. But when Ron Wolf took over as Packers general manager in 1991, boy, did he turn things around. Wolf replaced head coach Lindy Infante with Mike Holmgren. He traded a first-round pick to Atlanta for a backup quarterback named Brett Favre. The following year, he signed future Hall of Famer Reggie White as a free agent, and in 2000, a year before he retired, he traded for Ahman Green, who would become Green Bay's all-time leading rusher in 2009.

What did all this add up to? While Wolf was GM, the Packers posted seven consecutive winning seasons, from 1992 to 1998, and made six consecutive playoff appearances, from 1993 to 1998. The Packers twice won the NFC Championship and won their third Super Bowl in 1997.

# 72 THE TRADE

What would possess anyone to trade a first-round draft pick for a rookie quarterback who went 0-for-4 with two interceptions in his first season? That's what Packers GM Ron Wolf did in 1992. Wolf saw something few others saw in Brett Favre and went out and got him. You probably know the rest.

# 73 MIKE HOLMGREN

A quarter of a century of futility was completely unacceptable in Titletown. Over the next seven years, after Holmgren was hired as head coach in 1992, he guided the Packers to seven consecutive winning seasons, six playoff appearances, three Central Division titles, and two Super Bowl appearances, including their 35–21 victory over New England in Super Bowl XXXI. From 1992 to 1998, Holmgren's teams went 75–37 in regular season games and 9–5 in postseason games. He oversaw the maturation of Brett Favre, molding Favre into a three-time league MVP. But Holmgren's greatest legacy is returning the winning tradition to Green Bay.

Mike Holmgren, left, and Ron Wolf

Reggie White sacks Cincinnati's Jeff Blake, 1995.

# 74 THE MINISTER OF DEFENSE

The free agent signing of defensive end Reggie White in 1993 was a huge coup for Green Bay and changed the course of the franchise. The Packers defense had ranked 23rd in the league in 1992. In White's first season in Green Bay, the defense leaped to number two, and it became the top-ranked defense in the NFL in 1996. Not since 1967, the days of Vince Lombardi, had the Packers claimed that title.

Ordained at age 17, "the Minister of Defense" posted eight consecutive seasons of 10 sacks or more in Philadelphia before joining the Packers. In Green Bay, White notched four more seasons of 10 or more sacks, in 1993, 1995, 1997, and 1998, and tallied a total of 68 $1/2$ in six seasons—a franchise record at the time. He sacked New England quarterback Drew Bledsoe three times in the Packers' 35–21 win in Super Bowl XXXI. White was a Pro-Bowl selection all six years he was in Green Bay and 13 consecutive years over the course of his career. He was inducted into the Pro Football Hall of Fame in 2006.

# 75 PACKERS SACKERS

Kabeer Gbaja-Biamila, aka KGB, holds the all-time Green Bay sacks record with 74 $1/2$. In 2007, he broke Hall of Famer Reggie White's record of 68 $1/2$. Considered small for a defensive end at 250 pounds, Gbaja-Biamila is the only Packer to post 10 or more sacks in four consecutive seasons, from 2001 to 2004. He had 13 $1/2$ sacks in both 2001 and 2004.

Tim Harris holds the franchise record for sacks in a single season with 19 $1/2$, in 1989. Ezra Johnson is unofficially credited with 20 $1/2$ in 1978, but that was before the NFL began keeping official statistics on sacks. Vonnie Holliday holds the team record for sacks in a game with five, versus Buffalo, in 2002. Ezra Johnson (1978) and Dave Pureifory (1975) each recorded five sacks in a game before the stat became official.

## *"There wasn't a better teacher or mentor out there than Reggie White, on or off the field."*

—Brett Favre

*"Obviously talent gets you to a certain point, but it's what you do with it, how you handle it."*

–Brett Favre

# 76 THE GUNSLINGER

Brett Favre holds nearly every major NFL career passing record. His 508 touchdown passes (442 with Green Bay) are 88 more than second-place Dan Marino. He's the only player to surpass 10,000 pass attempts, 6,000 completions, and 70,000 passing yards. As a Packer, Favre threw for 300 or more yards in 55 games and surpassed 4,000 yards passing in a season five times. He was a nine-time Pro Bowl selection while in Green Bay and is the only player to win the NFL MVP award three consecutive years, from 1995 to 1997. And yet all that only tells part of the story.

From his first start in 1992, Favre's fearlessness imbued the Packers with grit and mettle that transformed the team. He steered the Packers to a 9–7 record that year—only the second winning season since 1972. Over the next 16 years, including 1992, Favre led the Packers to a 160–93 regular season record, seven division titles, 11 playoff appearances, two NFC Championships, and a Super Bowl win, in 1996.

The NFL has never seen another quarterback quite like him: with a cannon for an arm, an unquenchable will to win, unflinching leadership, and the gunslinger mentality that produced 43 career game-winning drives . . . and a handful of crushing defeats. Number 4 will forever be among the best ever to play the game.

"His accomplishments are legendary. And it's the passion with which he played that made everyone a Brett Favre fan."

–Ted Thompson, former Packers general manager

## 77 PLAYING CATCH

The first pass Brett Favre ever completed as a Packer, or as a pro for that matter, was to himself. Subbing for Don Majkowski in a 31–3 drubbing courtesy of the Tampa Bay Buccaneers, Favre's pass was batted in the air by Bucs defensive end Ray Seals. Favre caught it and was tackled by Seals for a seven-yard loss.

## 78 ALL GO

On September 20, 1992, the Packers trailed Cincinnati, 23–17, with 19 seconds left in the game. Things looked bleak for new coach Mike Holmgren, who was searching for his first win. Backup quarterback Brett Favre was playing in place of Don Majkowski, who was injured. Star receiver Sterling Sharpe had also left the game with an injury. Green Bay was still 35 yards from the end zone when Favre called "All Go," sending all three receivers streaking to the end zone. Reserve wideout Kitrick Taylor slipped past the cornerback, and Favre fired a dart to Taylor for the game-winning score. It was the only touchdown catch of Taylor's six-year career. The following week, Favre made the first of his record 253 consecutive starts with the Packers.

# 79 FATHER'S DAY

It was an amazing, inspired performance. Playing on the national stage on *Monday Night Football*, just a day after the death of his beloved father, Irv, Brett Favre gave the best performance of his spectacular career. In a late-December 2003 matchup with the Raiders in Oakland, and Green Bay fighting for a playoff spot, Favre threw for 399 yards and four touchdowns, compiling a career-best passer rating of 154.9. He was 22 of 30, with no interceptions, and threw scoring passes of 22, 23, 43, and 6 yards. Favre had seven completions of 20 yards or more as his receivers made one highlight-reel catch after another. The Packers pummeled the Raiders 41–7. And somewhere Irv Favre was smiling.

# 80 UNBREAKABLE

Perhaps the most impressive of all the records Brett Favre holds is his 298 consecutive games started (253 as a Packer). That's almost 19 full seasons without a day off.

# 81 SOMETHING ABOUT MARY

Brett Favre made a brief cameo appearance in the 1998 film *There's Something About Mary*. Favre, awkwardly playing himself, is one of many suitors of Cameron Diaz's Mary. Ted, played by Ben Stiller, had trouble with Favre's last name, memorably asking, "What about Brett Fav...ruh?"

## *"His record for most consecutive starts will never be broken. It's one of the most amazing records in sports. I guarantee you, he gets an immense amount of respect from every quarterback in the NFL for that record."*

—Former Bengals quarterback Carson Palmer, on Brett Favre

"*I know he was watching tonight.*"

—Brett Favre, speaking about his father, Irv

## 82 EARLY CHRISTMAS

Christmas Eve 1995. Snow flurries were flying and the Packers needed a win to secure a spot in the playoffs. Clinging to a 24–19 lead in the closing seconds, Packers cornerback Lenny McGill let Steelers receiver Yancey Thigpen shake loose for what appeared to be a game-winning touchdown catch. Except the wide-open Thigpen dropped the ball, giving Green Bay the victory and a welcome early Christmas gift.

## 83 SHARPE EDGE

Sterling Sharpe is one of the best receivers in Green Bay history and holds several team records. Had his career not been cut short by a neck injury in 1994, he may have been Green Bay's best ever. Sharpe led the NFL in receptions three times, in 1989, 1992, and 1993. Twice he led the league in touchdown receptions, in 1992 and 1994. From 1988 through 1994, Sharpe was the top Packers receiver in both receptions and receiving yards. His 595 catches are second best in Green Bay history. Sharpe holds the top two spots in the Packers record books for receptions in a season with 112 in 1993 and 108 in 1992. Both were NFL records at the time. His 18 touchdown catches in 1994 are also a team record and tied for third best in NFL history. The Packers inducted Sharpe, a five-time Pro Bowler, into the Packers Hall of Fame in 2002.

Sterling Sharpe

Pittsburgh's Yancey Thigpen drops a potential game-winning pass.

## 84 LEROY BUTLER

Butler overcame severe foot problems as a child that periodically required him to use a wheelchair. That type of determination helped Butler become one of the dominant defenders of his time. Butler played 12 seasons in Green Bay, and his 181 games played are the most by a defensive back in team history. When rookie head coach Mike Holmgren arrived in 1992, he switched Butler, originally a cornerback, to strong safety, and Butler flourished there. The four-time Pro-Bowler led or tied for the team lead in interception five times. He is the first defensive back in NFL history to tally 20 sacks and 20 interceptions. In the 1996 Super Bowl season, Butler recorded $6\frac{1}{2}$ sacks and five interceptions for Green Bay's league-best defense. He was also the originator of the famed Lambeau Leap. Butler was inducted into the Packers Hall of Fame in 2007.

## 85 THE LAMBEAU LEAP

It started innocently enough. Los Angeles Raiders quarterback Vince Evans, scrambling to escape pressure, tossed a swing pass to running back Randy Jordan, who was immediately hit by Packers safety LeRoy Butler near the Raiders' 40-yard line, causing Jordan to fumble. The loose ball was picked up by Green Bay's Reggie White, who rumbled toward the end zone. When White was corralled by Raiders lineman Steve Wisniewski, White lateraled the ball back to Butler, who sprinted in for the score from 25 yards out. Butler then spontaneously leaped into the arms of exultant fans—and a tradition was born. Robert Brooks and Antonio Freeman popularized the celebratory leap, but it was Butler who "invented" it in 1993.

*"The anticipation of all those fans ready to thank you for what you have done gives you chills like nothing else."*

—LeRoy Butler

LeRoy Butler leaps into he Lambeau Field crowd.

# 86 THE STREAK

Sandwiched between a 17–14 loss to the St. Louis Rams in their 1995 season opener and a 37–24 loss to Minnesota on October 5, 1998, the Packers ran off a streak of 25 consecutive regular season wins at Lambeau Field. It's the second-longest streak in NFL history; the Miami Dolphins won 27 in a row at home in the 1970s.

# 87 1996

It was an incredible year. The Packers motored through the regular season, getting off to an 8–1 start, then, after back-to-back losses in November, won five straight to finish the regular season 13–3. Along the way, Green Bay outscored its opponents 456–210. Both the offense and defense were ranked number one. Brett Favre threw for 3,899 yards and 39 touchdowns. And the Packers cruised to the NFC Central title. After easily dispatching San Francisco, 35–14, in the NFC divisional playoff, the Packers overcame a 17-degrees-below-zero wind chill and a gutsy effort by the upstart Carolina Panthers to win the NFC Championship, 30–13, and earn a berth in Super Bowl XXXI.

This page: From left, John Michels, Brett Favre, and Andre Rison celebrate a touchdown, 1996. Inset: Edgar Bennett (34) hurdles teammate Aaron Taylor.

Desmond Howard (81) returns a kickoff 99 yards for a touchdown in Super Bowl XXXI.

*"He's the best return guy I've ever seen."*
–Ron Wolf, on Desmond Howard

## 88 SUPER BOWL XXXI

Twenty-nine years had passed since the Packers last played in a Super Bowl—a 33–14 win over the Oakland Raiders in Super Bowl II, in 1968. No pressure. Brett Favre got Green Bay off to a quick start, connecting with Andre Rison on a 54-yard touchdown pass on the Packers' second play from scrimmage for an early 7–0 lead over New England. Just minutes later, the Packers led 10–0 on a Chris Jacke field goal that followed an interception by Doug Evans. The Patriots rallied to take a 14–10 lead as the first quarter ended, but Antonio Freeman hauled in a Favre bomb, scoring on an 81-yard catch-and-run to put the Packers back on top. Two more scores put the Packers up 27–14 at halftime. After the Patriots cut the lead to 27–21 in the third quarter, Desmond Howard returned the ensuing kickoff 99 yards for a touchdown—a Super Bowl record. The two-point conversion made it 35–21, and Green Bay held the Patriots scoreless the rest of the way. At last, the Lombardi Trophy was headed back to Titletown.

## 89 SUPER MAN

Desmond Howard won the 1991 Heisman Trophy in his senior year at Michigan. The Washington Redskins traded up to take him in the fourth spot overall in the 1992 draft. But Howard never blossomed into the receiver the Redskins hoped he would be. Still, after four lackluster seasons, including one in Jacksonville, Packers GM Ron Wolf thought Howard could be a difference maker in Green Bay. Wolf was right.

In 1996, Howard totaled 875 yards in punt returns during the regular season, shattering the NFL record of 692 yards. His 15.1-yard punt return average and three punt returns for touchdowns led the NFL. In an NFC divisional playoff game versus San Francisco, Howard returned one kick 71 yards for a touchdown and had a 46-yard return that set up another touchdown, in a 35–14 Packers win. Then, in the Super Bowl, with Green Bay clinging to a 6-point lead over the New England Patriots late in the third quarter, Howard returned the kickoff 99 yards for a touchdown that ultimately secured Green Bay's third Super Bowl title. Howard had 244 all-purpose yards in the game and was named Most Valuable Player.

## 90 AHMAN GREEN

When GM Ron Wolf traded underachieving cornerback Fred Vinson to Seattle for unproven running back Ahman Green in 2000, no one could have anticipated that Green would go on to become the Packers' all-time leading rusher. Green's 8,322 yards and 1,851 attempts are both team records. Six times he rushed for more than 1,000 yards in a season, including five straight years from 2000 to 2004. His 33 games of 100 or more yards rushing are also a team record.

Green's 2003 season stands out as the best in Packers history. That year, he rushed for 1,883 yards, including 10 games with 100 or more yards, and scored 20 touchdowns. In a December 28 contest versus Denver, Green tallied 218 yards rushing and scored on a 98-yard run—the longest in Green Bay history. All this while sharing the backfield with pass-happy Brett Favre.

> *"I didn't know he had the ball. I looked down and he got up and started running, and I'm thinking, 'What's he doing?' Then I just ran down there and jumped on him. Then I whispered in his ear, 'Did you catch it?'"*

—Brett Favre, on Antonio Freeman's game-winning catch

## 91 HE DID WHAT?

On a cold, drizzly November night in 2000, Antonio Freeman made one of the most improbable catches ever. With the score tied at 20–20, in overtime, the Minnesota Vikings' blitz forced Brett Favre to heave a prayer in Freeman's direction as he raced down the right sideline. Freeman slipped and fell to the ground face-first as he attempted to make the catch, giving Vikings cornerback Chris Dishman a free shot at an interception. Dishman bobbled the ball and appeared to knock it to the ground, but the ball bounced off Freeman's shoulder, and Freeman somehow spun over and got his hand under the ball, pulling it into his chest before it hit the ground. Thinking the pass had fallen incomplete, Dishman pranced in frustration while Freeman jumped up and dashed into the end zone for a game-winning touchdown.

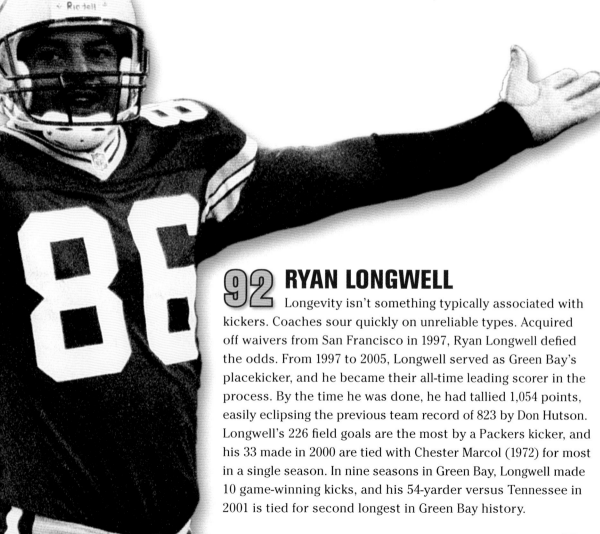

## 92 RYAN LONGWELL

Longevity isn't something typically associated with kickers. Coaches sour quickly on unreliable types. Acquired off waivers from San Francisco in 1997, Ryan Longwell defied the odds. From 1997 to 2005, Longwell served as Green Bay's placekicker, and he became their all-time leading scorer in the process. By the time he was done, he had tallied 1,054 points, easily eclipsing the previous team record of 823 by Don Hutson. Longwell's 226 field goals are the most by a Packers kicker, and his 33 made in 2000 are tied with Chester Marcol (1972) for most in a single season. In nine seasons in Green Bay, Longwell made 10 game-winning kicks, and his 54-yarder versus Tennessee in 2001 is tied for second longest in Green Bay history.

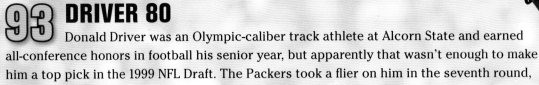

## 93 DRIVER 80

Donald Driver was an Olympic-caliber track athlete at Alcorn State and earned all-conference honors in football his senior year, but apparently that wasn't enough to make him a top pick in the 1999 NFL Draft. The Packers took a flier on him in the seventh round, and Driver proved more than worthy of the leap of faith. In 2011, Driver became the all-time Green Bay leader in total receiving yards as well as receptions. He led the team in receptions six times and had seven seasons of 1,000 or more receiving yards, including six in a row from 2004 to 2009. Driver's nine seasons in a row with 50 or more receptions, from 2002 to 2010, is a team record. During that period, Driver had at least one reception in 133 consecutive regular season games. Driver is currently fourth all-time in touchdown receptions with 59 and is a four-time Pro Bowler.

## 94 WE WANT THE BALL

After a tense, seesaw battle between Green Bay and Seattle resulted in a 27–27 tie at the end of regulation in a 2003–4 NFC wild-card game, Seattle quarterback and former Favre understudy Matt Hasselback announced, upon winning the coin toss for overtime, "We want the ball and we're going to score." The referee was wearing a microphone for the toss, and Hasselback's bold declaration was heard throughout Lambeau Field and on television. On Seattle's second possession of overtime, Packers defensive back Al Harris intercepted a Hasselback pass and returned it 52 yards for the game-winning touchdown. It was the first overtime game in NFL history won by a defensive touchdown. It seems that Harris wanted the ball more.

Donald Driver makes a spectacular reception versus San Francisco.

## 95 MIKE McCARTHY

In his second season as head coach of the Packers, in 2007, McCarthy led the team to the NFC Championship Game, where the Packers lost to New York, 23–20, in overtime, following a Brett Favre interception—Favre's last pass as a Packer. McCarthy then managed the awkward transition from Favre to Aaron Rodgers, and three years later, McCarthy led the Packers back to the Super Bowl. In a display of brash confidence, or bravado, McCarthy had the players fitted for championship rings … the night before the game. His players didn't disappoint, delivering a 31–25 win over the Pittsburgh Steelers.

## 96 WHITE HOUSE

President Obama had announced that he would attend Super Bowl XLV if Chicago won the 2010 NFC Championship. Packers cornerback Charles Woodson took notice. In his locker room speech following Green Bay's 21–14 victory over the Bears, Woodson commanded, "I want y'all to think about one thing … one. For two weeks, think about one. Let's be one mind, let's be one heartbeat, for one purpose, one goal, for one more game … one. Let's get it. And check this, if the president doesn't want to come watch us in the Super Bowl … guess what? We'll go see him! Let's get a 'White House' on three. One, two, three, White House!"

Charles Woodson (21) breaks up a pass intended for Pittsburgh's Mike Wallace during Super Bowl XLV. Inset: Charles Woodson presents President Obama with a Packers stock certificate during a ceremony at the White House.

Clay Matthews sacks Carolina quarterback Cam Newton (1).

# 97 MANE MAN

Flying around the field like a modern-day Thor, with long, golden locks streaming from beneath his helmet, Packers linebacker Clay Matthews strikes fear into opposing offenses with his thunderous strength and lightning speed. Matthews has quite a football pedigree—his grandfather, father, and uncle all played in the NFL before him. He is the first Packer voted to the Pro Bowl in his first two seasons since John Brockington in 1971–72. And Matthews' 13 ½ sacks in 2010 were the most by a Packer and fourth best in the league. And yet, it's his hair that often gets the most attention. Matthews says it's representative of the wild man he becomes on the field. Anyone who has seen him play would have to agree.

"You let the hair down and that's
when the wild man comes out."
– Clay Matthews

"Green Bay wanted me, and I'm forever grateful for that and hopefully will repay them with another trophy in the case."

–Aaron Rodgers

# 98 AARON RODGERS

Rodgers was anointed heir apparent to Brett Favre when he was drafted out of the University of California in 2005. And so the waiting began. For three seasons, Rodgers mostly sat while Favre continued to add to his legend. When Favre decided to call it quits—sort of—in 2008, Rodgers finally got his chance.

In his first season at the helm, in 2009, Rodgers led the Packers to an 11–5 regular season record and a berth in the NFC playoffs as a wild card. The following year, Rodgers guided the Packers back into the playoffs, again as a wild card, and then steered Green Bay to three straight wins in the hostile environs of Philadelphia, Atlanta, and Chicago. The Packers' 21–14 win over the Bears in the NFC Championship Game earned Green Bay a berth in Super Bowl XLV versus the mighty Steelers. There, Rodgers shredded the vaunted Pittsburgh defense for 304 passing yards and three touchdowns, earning him the game's MVP award and the Packers' fourth Lombardi Trophy.

In 2011, Rodgers threw for a Packers' record 4,643 yards and 45 TDs. Rodgers' 122.5 passer rating set the NFL single season record. The Packers won the NFC North crown and a third consecutive berth in the playoffs.

Clay Matthews, left, and Aaron Rodgers celebrate the Packers' Super Bowl XLV victory.

# 99 SUPER BOWL XLV

This was a battle between NFL dynasties. The six-time Super Bowl champion Pittsburgh Steelers faced off against 12-time NFL champion Green Bay at Cowboys Stadium in Arlington, Texas, on February 6, 2011. With two touchdown passes by Aaron Rodgers and a 37-yard interception return by Nick Collins for another touchdown, the Packers surged to a 21–10 halftime lead. But the gritty Steelers battled back in the second half, cutting Green Bay's lead to 28–25 midway through the fourth quarter. Rodgers then methodically drove the Packers down the field to the Steelers' 6, where Green Bay had to settle for a 23-yard field goal and a six-point lead with just over two minutes to play. The Packers defense then shut down Pittsburgh's last drive, and Green Bay claimed its fourth Super Bowl title and record 13th NFL Championship.

Packers fans celebrate a touchdown with Matt Flynn (10).

# 100 IN LIKE FLYNN

With the number one seed in the NFC playoff secured, backup quarterback Matt Flynn was given the start, in place of Aaron Rodgers, in Green Bay's 2011 regular season finale against Detroit. Flynn, who had thrown only five passes all season prior to the Lions game, went 31 for 44, and set team records with 480 yards passing and six touchdowns, including a 4-yarder to Jermichael Finley with 1:10 remaining, which gave the Packers a 45–41 victory. Four of Flynn's touchdown passes were 35 yards or longer, including an 80-yard screen pass to Ryan Grant—the longest reception by a Packers running since Elijah Pitts had an 80-yard touchdown catch versus the Rams in 1966.

# 101 ALMOST PERFECT

In 2011, the Packers built on the momentum from their six-game winning streak the previous season, capped by their win in Super Bowl XLV. Green Bay raced to a 13–0 start and had a legitimate shot at only the second perfect 16–0 regular season record in NFL history. But in one of the biggest upsets of the year, Kansas City shocked the Packers and the sports world with a 19–14 win, spoiling the perfect season. Despite the loss, the Packers' 19-game winning streak, including the playoffs, is the second-longest in NFL history. Green Bay went on to finish with a franchise-best 15–1 mark, setting several franchise records, including 560 total points scored—an average of 35 points per game.

Aaron Rodgers
Inset: Packers stock
owner Steve Tate

# ACKNOWLEDGMENTS

It takes quite a team effort to see a project like this through to completion. I had the great pleasure of working with a select few who helped immensely in bringing this book to life.

Mary Tiegreen conceived this series of books and has been the guiding force in their development and success. For this and her continued inspiration and support, a special note of thanks. She and her husband, Hubert, have become more than good friends. They have become part of our family...and we wouldn't have it any other way.

To my editor, Jennifer Levesque, and her team—managing editor Jen Graham, copy editor Richard Slovak, production manager Tina Cameron, and assistant editor Wesley Royce—please take a bow. You are indispensable. Thanks for all you do.

One of my favorite parts of compiling these books is finding the images that so beautifully complement the text. For that, I owe a debt of gratitude to Yvette Reyes and her associates at AP Images, as well as Kevin Kelly at Getty Images.

To everyone involved with the Green Bay Packers franchise, past and present, your sustained commitment to success and community service is a model for all. Thank you.

And to all you Packers fans out there, stand and cheer. You are the lifeblood of the team, the true reason for all of this. The green and gold. Bravo!

Lastly, to my family, I cherish you all. None of this would be possible without your continuing love and support. Cheers!